The Surname Darvill

Susan Morris &
Wendy Bosberry-Scott

The question of surnames, their origins, distribution and history, lies at the heart of genealogy as well as being fascinating in its own right.

In the 1980s and 1990s, long before many genealogical sources were even indexed, let alone online, our Surname Report service provided expert assessments of the origins, history and distribution of selected British surnames, using the sources available at the time.

Now, with so many more sources available, we believe that these reports retain their value as studies of individual surnames, and so we are gradually making the Debrett Surname Archive available online and in print for the first time. Some modern indexes have been consulted to refresh and update the reports.

Debrett Ancestry Research Ltd, PO Box 379,
Winchester SO23 9YQ
Tel: 01962 841904
Email: info@debrettancestry.co.uk
Website: www.debrettancestry.co.uk

CONTENTS

Overview

The use of surnames in England began in the Norman period, when surnames were not necessarily hereditary but usually a form of description. Some described the individual's trade or profession; others were nicknames; some gave the father's Christian name; others gave the individual's place of residence or origin.

Different surnames might be used in different documents, or more than one surname given in one document. Early descriptions were fairly elaborate and by the thirteenth and fourteenth centuries these were simpler, but still variable, and indeed the instability of surnames continued until well into the seventeenth century.

Although some Normans would already have had hereditary surnames on their arrival in Britain, the passing on of a surname from generation to generation only became customary in Britain gradually during the course of the thirteenth and fourteenth centuries. At the end of this period most of the population apparently had surnames.

Variations in the spelling of a family's surname continue to be found until the present century. Before this, as most people could not read or write, the parish clerk or other official would write down the name as they heard it.

There are four main groups of surnames:

A Local names, which describe a person by his place of residence or origin.

B Occupational names, which describe a person by his trade or profession.

C Surnames of relationship, which refer to the Christian name of the father or other important relative.

D Nicknames or sobriquets, coined to describe a person in terms of his appearance or character.

Many surnames have uncertain origins, but the name Darvill clearly falls into Category A. Darval(l), Darvile, Dearville, Dervall, Derville, Dorvell, Dorville, Darfield, Derfield, Darwall, Darwell, Dorwall and Dur(i)val have all been regarded as variants of the name.

Origins and Early Examples

The authoritative *Dictionary of British Surnames,* edited by P H Reaney and updated by R M Wilson, includes the name Darvill in the edition of 1995. The name is grouped with the variants listed above. The entry suggests that these names originate from one of three place names, all found multiply in northern France: Orville (Orne, Pas-de-Calais), Urvill (Auche, Calvados, La Manche) or Orival (Charente, Seine-Maritime, Somme); and that it is 'impossible to separate out the forms'. The meaning of all these names would seem to be 'golden town'.

The Larousse *Dictionnaire de Noms et Prénoms de France* also suggests the Normandy villages of d'Arville and Arville as possible places of origin for the French surname Darville.

M A Lower's *Patronymica Brittanica,* an early but still interesting surname dictionary published in 1860, noted that Darvell or Darvill was the name of an estate near Battle in Sussex; but Lower guessed that the surname Dorville probably stems from one of two villages named Douville in Normandy. 'Darvel' survives as a local name in the parish of Brightling, East Sussex, and is also the name of a Scottish town, but Lower was probably correct in suggesting that these place names are unconnected to the surname.

Several medieval examples of possible variants of the surname Darvill, have been found in English records (cited by Reaney unless otherwise indicated), but none of these is very close to the modern form of the name:

1130	Robert de Aureavalle Devon Pipe Rolls	
	(*The Norman People*)	
1201	Robert de Durevill	Somerset Assizes
c1272	Walter Dorival Hundred Rolls	
	(*The Norman People*)	
1300	Hugh Durival	Eynsham, Oxford
1332	Sibill Doryual	Sussex Subsidy Rolls

The earliest two examples include the preposition 'de', indicating a place-name origin. By the fourteenth century the practice of adding 'de' before the name appears to have been dropped, which was consistent with the general development of surnames at this time.

Distribution

In 1890 H B Guppy published his *Homes of Family Names in Great Britain*, still the only published work on surname distribution in Britain as a whole. His work was based on printed genealogies and a survey of county directories for the 1880s, in which he looked especially at the names of farmers, reasoning that they were among the most stable groups in society. He noted that there was a proportion of 40 in 10,000 farmers who used the name Darvell or Darvill in Buckinghamshire at that time. Guppy restricted his study to names which appeared in a proportion of 7:10,000 or higher. Buckinghamshire was the only county in which the name was found in significant numbers.

Guppy stated that the name had been found in Buckinghamshire in the seventeenth century and gave two examples: Thomas Darvell of Wendover in 1656 and William Darvell of Langley in 1699.

Anecdotal evidence from online genealogy forums suggests that the names Dorrell and Darville interchanged in Buckinghamshire.

George F Black's dictionary of *The Surnames of Scotland* refers to the name Dervail. This is an Anglicised version of the Gaelic name *Diorbhail* which had been spelt 'Derval' in the book 'Dean of Lismore' by the poet McGillinduk. The early Gaelic spelling is *Deirbheile* which he translated as meaning 'grief, trouble of mind'.

This name is probably unconnected with the English surname Darvill.

Many of the sources available for charting surname distribution through the centuries are necessarily confined to the wealthier sectors of the population: in general, nobody wanted to know the names of the poor but the names of those with money or land were naturally of interest to the authorities. However, one source that covers the whole of the social spectrum is provided by English parish registers, the earliest of which began in 1538 following a mandate that all parish priests should keep a weekly record of all baptisms, marriages and burials that took place in their parish.

A pre-digital survey of a cross section of parish registers for the years 1601 and 1602 was carried out in 1910 by F K and S Hitching; incidences of a particular surname are noted by parish and county, although with no indication of numbers of references. Derville was noted as appearing in the registers of the Walloon Church in Canterbury, Kent (used by Protestant immigrants from Europe) but did not appear elsewhere in the survey, indicating a relatively uncommon name.

The modern *FamilySearch* database of English parish register entries (which is large but not comprehensive) shows no Darvill/Darvell entries at all for the period 1538 to 1599; there are just two entries for the form Dervill, both from Great Bentley in Essex (where Laurance and Avise Dervill were buried in May 1563); and a single entry for the form Dervall in this period, this being from Southampton (Marye, daughter of Hewe Dervall, was baptised on 15 January 1593). However, this partly reflects the general sparseness of records for this early period.

A search of the National Archives *Discovery Catalogue*, which covers a vast and miscellaneous collection of documents from around the United Kingdom, shows no instances of the surname Darvill as such for the pre-1600 period, but Darvill appears as a place name in a Chancery case dated 1544–1551 between John Neville, Lord Latimer, and Sir Anthony Wyngefelde, knight. It is not clear from the catalogue entry where Darvill was, but it appears among Staffordshire place names.

The name Darvel(l) appears in a handful of entries in the *Discovery Catalogue* for the pre-1600 period, including the following item, which is the earliest example we have found to the specific form Darvill/Darvell, if the catalogue entry is correct:

> Sir Edward Darvell Knight to Wm Sharington
> Receipt for £40 in part of payment for purchase of yearly rent from certain lands in Co Wilts. 14 February 1545 - *Northamptonshire Record Office W(A) box 2/parcel V/no.3/b3*

W A Shaw's *Knights of England* (1906) does not mention a Sir Edward Darvell but it is possible that this receipt refers to Sir Edward Darrell, who was knighted in 1544 at Leith, Edinburgh. Shaw does list two nineteenth-century knights: Henry Darvill (1883) and John B Darvall (1877).

A useful guide to the distribution of surnames for the sixteenth, seventeenth and eighteenth centuries in England is provided by the indexes to wills proved, and administrations granted, at the Prerogative Court of (the Archbishop of) Canterbury, in London, which had superior jurisdiction over local ecclesiastical courts where wills were proved until 1858. The PCC thus provides a national index, although it is not a completely representative one, as testators whose wills were proved in the PCC were mostly among the wealthier members of society, and a disproportionate number of them were from London or Middlesex.

The online indexes for the earliest period (1384 to 1583) shows no entries for the name Darvill, Darvell, Dervill, Dervall, Dearville, Darwall, Darwell, Dervill(e), Dorvill(e) or Dorwal(l), reflecting the general picture provided by the parish register surveys, that this was an uncommon name in this early period.

A search of the printed indexes for the years 1584 to 1604; 1605 to 1619; 1620 to 1629; 1653 to 1656; 1661 to 1670; 1676 to 1685; and 1750 to 1800 found the following entries for Dearville, Darvall, Darvell, Darvile, Darvill, Darwall, Darwell, Dervall, Dervill(e) Dorvell, Dorvill(e) and Dorwall:

Sixteenth Century
1587   Hughe Dervall, town of Southants

Seventeenth Century
1618   George Dearville, taking a journey to Ireland, from Harrow on the Hill, Middlesex
1631   John Darvall of St Mary Southampton
1656   Warde Dorwall, husb[andman], Veny Castle, Wookey, Somerset
1659   Richard Dorvell, husb[andman], Hembridge, East Pennard, Somerset

1659 Thomas Darvell, widower, Underwick, Scotland

1660 Margaret Dorvell, wid[ow] Ditcheatt, Somerset

1667 Abraham Darvill, carpenter, St Giles, Cripplegate, Middlesex

1668 James Dorville, Abbas Rothing, Essex

1674 Dorothy Dervall, widdowe of Flower Street, Stebonheath, Middlesex

1679 John Darvell, naylesmith, Wapping St Mary, als[o] Whitechapel Middlesex

1692 Benjamin Darvile, mar[riner], bachelor, St Paul, Shadwell, Middlesex - HMS St Michael

1694 Peter Darvall, Raymills, Maidenhead, Berkshire

Eighteenth Century

1750 Gideon Le Duchat De Dorville Esq., Pts

1751 John Dorville, Pts

1753 Mary De Bonneval Derville, Middlesex

1754 Elizabeth Darvill, Buckinghamshire

1755 James Darwell, Pts and Surrey

1763 John Darvill, Surrey

1763 Sara Maria Dorville, Pts

1763 William Darvill, Pts

1764 Hannah Darvell, Oxon.

1767 Peter Darvall, Berkshire

1768 Ann Darvill, Surrey

1771 Jean Le Duchat De Dorville Esq., Pts

1771 Deborah Darvall, Middlesex

1772 Richard Darvill, Middlesex

1774 Mary Darvall, London

1780 Stephen Darvell, Middlesex

1782 Joseph Darvell, Buckinghamshire

1784 John Darvill, Buckinghamshire

1787 Elizabeth Darvill, Berkshire

1787 Thomas Darvill, Berkshire

1790 Richard Darvill, Middlesex

1796   Arthur Dorvell, Kent

1799   John Dorville Esq., Middlesex

1799   Susanna or Susan Darville, Middlesex

Nineteenth Century

1800   Honor Darwall, spinster of Newport, Shropshire

1800   Elizabeth Darvel, spinster of St Clement Danes, Middlesex

1800   Lady Philippina D'Orville, widow of Utrecht

1805   John Darvill, common brewer of Bledlow, Buckinghamshire

1810   Hon Joan Fredri(c)k D'Orville, late President Magistrate and member of the Council of this city and Director of the East India Company of Amsterdam, Holland

1813   James Darvall otherwise Darvill, labourer of Chepping Wycombe, Buckinghamshire

1814   Margaret Darwall, widow of Walsall, Staffordshire

1815   James Darvell, victualler of Beech Street, Barbican, London

1820   John William Dorville, 1 John Street, America Square, London

1825   George Philip Dorville, merchant of John Street, America Square, London

1835   Elizabeth Darvell, widow of Coleshill, Hertfordshire

1839   Peter Darvell, gardener of Maidstone, Kent

1839   Ann Dorville, of Clapham, Surrey

1840   Richard Darvill, late veterinary surgeon of 7th Hussars now on half pay of Bristol

1841   Thomas Dorville, Lt Col in the army of St James', Middlesex

1843   Charles Henry Darwall, gentleman of Walsall, Staffordshire

1844   Thomas Darwell, merchant of Manchester, Lancashire

1844   Elizabeth Dorville, widow of Alphington, Devon

1848   Jacob Darvell, Coachmaker of Wokingham, Berkshire

1850   Frederick Derville, Lt Col commandant in military service of the East India Company, of 22 Bolton Street, Piccadilly, Middlesex

1853   Sarah Dervall, widow of Faversham, Kent

1853   Elizabeth Dorville, spinster of Hammersmith, Middlesex

1855   James Darvill, draper and miller of Farnham, Surrey

1855   Mary Dorville, spinster of Hammersmith, Middlesex

1856   Rev Frederick William Darwall, minister and clerk of Sholden, Kent

1857   Mary Ann Darvill, spinster of 17 Charlotte Street, Park Street, Bristol

The PCC was the usual court used for testators who died abroad and there are examples of that happening in this list; those marked 'Pts', meaning *in partibus transmarinis* died abroad or at sea. The reference to a Scottish testator is unusual for this court.

It is interesting to see that the earliest reference, to the testator Hughe Dervall of Southampton (1587) is from the same town as our earliest parish register example (Hewe Dervall baptised a daughter Mary in Southampton in 1593), though clearly these two entries relate to different men.

The specific form Darvill appears only sporadically throughout the whole period covered by the PCC indexes (1384–1858), with a total of 15 examples. Six of these are from the London area. There are just six examples of the close variant Darvell, three of which are from London or nearby. The form Darvall appears in a further 15 examples, five of which are from London or Middlesex.

The names Jean and Gideon Le Duchat De Dorville and Mary De Bonneval Derville are so unanglicised that they must have come to England much later than the Norman invasion. The reference to a Derville worshipping at the Walloon Church in Canterbury (Canterbury being an important Huguenot centre) at the beginning of the seventeenth century is further evidence that families of this name came to England as immigrants in the seventeenth century or later, probably as Protestant refugees.

When the French and those who died abroad are removed from the above list of PCC wills, we are left with a large number of examples of the surname from Middlesex, and this is to some extent explained by the fact that the court was situated in London and was often used by local people, especially in the later period.

There are also four items from Berkshire (Darvill/Darvall) in the late seventeenth and eighteenth centuries and a Darvell in the nineteenth century; three from Surrey (Darwell/Darvill/Darvel); and three from Buckinghamshire (Darvill/Darvall) in the second half of the eighteenth century and one Darvill at the very beginning of the nineteenth century with a Darvall in 1813. In the seventeenth century there is also a small cluster of three Dorwall/Dorvells in Somerset and two early examples from Hampshire (Dervall, Darvall). In addition to this there are isolated examples from

Shropshire, Oxfordshire and Essex. The overall picture is of a concentration in the south east of England but also a significant group in Somerset.

There are two examples of D'Orville in the list, both from Holland and probably relating to a husband and wife. However, the variant Dorville is found in Devon and in Middlesex and Surrey, with one example of Derville in Middlesex. Darwall is found in Staffordshire and Kent.

For the nineteenth century, H B Guppy's survey has been mentioned above. Another important Victorian source is the *Return of Owners of Land* of 1873, sometimes known as the Modern Domesday Book. This source lists, county by county, every owner of an acre of land or more, with their residence (not necessarily the address of their property) and the acreage of their holding.

Return of Owners of Land

Berkshire	1	Darvill
Buckinghamshire	4	Darvell
	4	Darvill
Hertfordshire	1	Darvill
Lancashire	1	Darwell
Montgomeryshire	1	Darwell
Salop	1	Darville
Southampton	2	Darvill
Surrey	2	Darvill

Darvill(e), Darvell and Darwell are the only examples found in this list. Buckinghamshire has the highest numbers with four listings each for Darvell and Darvill and this supports Guppy's findings. The entries for

Berkshire, Southampton and Surrey recall the picture shown by the PCC will lists, but there are more far-flung references here to Wales (perhaps related to the Shropshire example here and in the PCC list) and Lancashire.

The first decennial census return in England, Scotland and Wales was taken in 1801, but personal information was only recorded from 1841 onwards. From 1851, the age, occupation and birthplace is given for each member of the household, and so these records provide invaluable genealogical information as well as a fascinating 'snapshot' of the family in the nineteenth century. The latest return currently open to public inspection is that of 1911 and there are now national indexes to the returns from 1841 onwards, although these indexes are not wholly reliable. Using these indexes, we found the following numbers for Darvill, Darvell, Darvall and Dorville in Channel Islands, England, Scotland (not 1911) and Wales:

> 6 June 1841 – Darvill (371), Darvell (143), Darvall (10), Dorville (1)
> 30 March 1851 – Darvill (368), Darvell (165), Darvall (12), Dorville (7)
> 7 April 1861 – Darvill (444), Darvell (188), Darvall (17), Dorville (4)
> 2 April 1871 – Darvill (583), Darvell (162), Darvall (22), Dorville (4)
> 3 April 1881 – Darvill (621), Darvell (297), Darvall (43), Dorville (5)
> 5 April 1891 – Darvill (586), Darvell (204), Darvall (20)
> 31 March 1901 – Darvill (816), Darvell (221), Darvall (34), Dorville (8)
> 2 April 1911 – Darvill (895), Darvell (439), Darvall (59), Dorville (14)

There were no entries for this name at all in the Channel Islands in any year and only three Darvells in Scotland in 1901. There was only one entry for the name Darvill in the 1881, 1901 and 1911 with nothing for this name in 1891. The name appeared in Scotland in 1871 as Darvill but there were only six entries.

In 1881 the name appeared in Scotland and Wales as Darvall but only in very small numbers: one in Scotland and three in Wales. Dorville was by far the rarest of the variants with no showing of the name at all in the 1901 census; and it was only found in England.

Overall, the surname is not a common one in any census record with less than 2000 entries for the surname, in any form, showing in the 1911 census.

Famous bearers of the name

No family of the name Darvill (or a variant thereof) has achieved the distinction of inclusion in the *Dictionary of National Biography* for the British Isles or in lists of peers, baronets or 'landed gentry'. However, in recent years the actor Arthur Darvill (born 1982) has become well-known through his appearance in TV programmes such as *Dr Who* and *Broadchurch*.

There are three coats of arms listed in Burke's *General Armory,* granted to men of the name Darvall, Darwell and Dervill.

> **Darvall** - Gules on a pale or, between four bezants, a lion rampant of the field. *Crest* - A lion's head or, collared gules charged with three bezants.

> **Darwell** - Argent three anchors in pale sable between two palots vert a chief gules *Crest* - A lion's head erased or, ducally crowned gules

> **Dervill** - Gules a lion rampant and a fleur-de-lis argent

No references have been found to printed genealogies of Darvill or variant families.

Summary

To conclude, the name Darvill appears to be one of a group of related surnames of French origin deriving ultimately from one of a number of locations in northern France. However, the specific form Darvill appears to have been a late arrival on the scene, and we have found no examples of this precise form prior to the seventeenth century. The earliest close variant (Dervill, 1563) comes from the parish of Great Bentley in Essex where the names of the two parishioners (Laurance and Avise) suggest that they too might have been recent arrivals in the country. This all suggests that the specific form of the surname Darvill, and its close variants Dervill and Dervall, might have arrived in England, not as part of the Norman invasion, but with Protestant immigrants in the sixteenth century.

Having arrived in England, the name and its variants seem to have remained fairly consistently rooted in the south and south-east of the country, especially in Berkshire, Buckinghamshire and Middlesex.

Sources

P H Reaney, *The Origins of English Surnames* (London: Routledge & Kegan Paul, 1967)

P H Reaney & R M Wilson, *A Dictionary of British Surnames* (Oxford: Oxford University Press, 3rd edition, 1995)

P H Reaney, *Dictionary of British Surnames* (London: Routledge & Kegan Paul, 2nd edition, 1976)

P Hanks & F Hodges, *A Dictionary of Surnames* (Oxford University Press, 1988)

M A Lower, *Patronymica Brittanica* (London, 1860)

C W Bardsley, *Dictionary of English and Welsh Surnames* (1901: reprinted, Baltimore: Genealogical Publishing Co, 1967)

C L'Estrange Ewen, *Guide to the Origin of British Surnames* (London: John Gifford, 1938)

H B Guppy, Homes of Family Names in Great Britain (London, 1890)

Ernest Weekley, *The Romance of Names* (London: John Murray, 2nd edition, 1917)

Ernest Weekley, *Surnames* (London: John Murray, 1917)

George F Black, *The Surnames of Scotland* (New York Public Library, 1946)

Edward McLysaght, *The Surnames of Ireland* (Dublin: Irish University Press, 1977)

T J & Prys Morgan, *Welsh Surnames* (Cardiff: University of Wales Press, 1985)

F K & S Hitching, *References to English Surnames in 1601* (Walton on Thames: Bernau, 1910)

F K & S Hitching, *References to English Surnames in 1602* (Walton on Thames: Bernau, 1911)

Debrett's People of Today (Debrett's Peerage Limited: London, 1996)

The Oxford Dictionary of National Biography (online, 2004–2014)

The Concise Dictionary of National Biography, Part II, 1901–1950, (Oxford, 1961)

Burke's Family Index (London: Burke's Peerage Limited, 1976)

H R Moulton, *Palaeography, Genealogy & Topography* (Sale Catalogue, 1930)

Index to Prerogative Court of Canterbury Wills (The National Archives: online)

G W Marshall, *The Genealogist's Guide* (1903; reprinted, Baltimore: GPC 1973)

J B Whitmore, *A Genealogical Guide* (London, 1953)

Charles Bridge, *An Index to Pedigrees* (London, 1867)

Geoffrey B Barrow, *The Genealogist's Guide* (London: Research Publishing Co, 1977)

Sir Bernard Burke, *The General Armory* (London, 1884)

C R Humphrey-Smith, editor, *Burke's General Armory Volume II,* (Tabard Press, 1973)

The Return of Owners of Land (1873)

Eilert Ekwall, *The Concise Oxford Dictionary of English Place-Names* (Oxford: Clarendon Press, 4th edition, 1960)

E G Withycombe, *The Oxford Dictionary of English Christian Names* (Oxford: Clarendon Press, 2nd edition, 1950)

W J Hardy & W Page, A Calendar to the Feet of Fines for London and Middlesex: Vol 1 Richard I – Richard III (1189–1485) (London, 1892)

Richard McKinley, *The Surnames of Oxfordshire* (English Surnames Series III: Leopard's Head Press, 1977)

Richard McKinley, *The Surnames of Sussex* (English Surnames Series V: Leopard's Head Press, 1988)

Richard McKinley, *The Surnames of Lancashire* (English Surnames Series IV: Leopard's Head Press, 1981)

Richard McKinley, *Norfolk and Suffolk Surnames in the Middle Ages* (English Surnames Series II: Phillimore, 1975)

George Redmonds, *Yorkshire West Riding* (English Surnames Series I: Phillimore, 1973)

The Norman People (London, 1874)

Debrett's Heraldry (London, 1933)

J P Brooke-Little, revised, *Boutell's Heraldry* (Frederick Warne: London, 1970)

Indexes to 1841–1911 Census Returns of England and Wales (The National Archives/*Ancestry.com*)

ScotlandsPeople: Indexes to Old Parish Registers, Testaments, Statutory Registers